Little Book of Godly Affirmations

Chere l Claxton

ISBN 978-93-5610-608-6
© Chere l Claxton 2022
Published in India 2022 by Pencil

A brand of

One Point Six Technologies Pvt. Ltd.
123, Building J2, Shram Seva Premises,
Wadala Truck Terminal, Wadala (E)
Mumbai 400037, Maharashtra, INDIA
E connect@thepencilapp.com
W www.thepencilapp.com

Author biography

I HAVE READ MANY SELF-HELP BOOKS OVER THE PAST TEN YEARS FOR HEALTH CONDITIONS AND PERSONAL DEVELOPMENT.

I HAVE COMPLETED A DIPLOMA CERTIFICATE COURSE IN PERSONAL DEVELOPMENT STAGE 2/3

I HAVE PUBLISHED BOOKS ONLINE PLEASE CHECK OUT MY BOOKS ON KINDLE SUCH AS AFFIRMATIONS FOR POSITIVE CHANGE

CONTENTS

Introduction

Introduction Affirmations are and how they can help you the benefits of Affirmations

Affirmations are Positive Statements to help you challenge and overcome self-sabotage and negative thoughts using affirmations to drive positive change and re-program your thinking patterns over time you will begin to think and act differently in a more God-centered way.

Affirmations are like exercises for our mind and outlook and improve our chances of success.

Affirmations can be used as a treatment and work well alongside other treatments thus complementing it.
It may take some time to notice any changes so patience will be required and persistence to reach the desired outcome.

Take back control of your thoughts and begin altering these thought patterns.
Altering these thought patterns produce a positive outlook and you become more focused on your creator.
You may want to use affirmations to control negative feelings.
Improve your productivity or keep your motivation.

You may want to use these affirmations for behaviour change and use these affirmations to assist you in that process.

Affirmations are a self-help tool for a successful Strategy.

Affirmations can help strengthen self-worth by boosting your positive opinion of yourself.

Use these affirmations for god focusing on these positive statements to promote self-confidence.

Affirmations generally work as a tool for shifting your mindset.

Affirmations help you to achieve your goals.

Affirmations encourage your brain to take these positive affirmations as fact with true belief.

Believing in your own ability with God's help and assistance reminds you that you are not alone.

There is indeed a higher source that we can use in a positive way to boost optimism and improve mood.

Allowing yourself to focus away from perceived failure and inadequacies directing your focus toward God's given Strengths to you.

Practising affirmations may help you feel more relaxed and help you get through stressful moments.

You may want to add these affirmations after prayer.

Affirmations then are serving as an additional resource.

Affirmations can be used to help you overcome self-doubt decrease stress and become more open to behaviour change and a positive outlook.

Affirmation may broaden your overall perception of what God thinks of you rather than what others think or say about you.

Affirmations can reduce the effects of negative emotions reducing reactivity and regulating emotions.

Self-affirmations work by priming the regions of ventrolateral prefrontal cortex.

Affirmations are effective due to Neuroplasticity or the re-wiring of the brain.

Our brains are constantly re-wiring themselves and building new neural pathways.

Affirmations are one way to re-wire to think more positive.

Positive affirmations tell us that we are still doing well and that we should not give up hope.

Affirmations can give us momentum to not give up hope helping us build resilience and giving us an extra boost.

Affirmations can prevent us from ruminating over negative thoughts and situations.

Affirmations can encourage positive happy feelings thoughts and attitudes God intends us to be Joyful.

Affirmations challenge unhelpful thinking and are a helpful resource when you need support and reassurance from God this may reduce your sensitivity to threats.

Affirmations help build awareness support your well-being and encourage emotional stability.

Affirmations can inspire creativity and breakthrough limiting beliefs instilling hope for the future and encouraging a sense of calm helping you to be present with God at that moment.

Affirmations help you overcome inner barriers.

Affirmations create a positive perception of who you are and instil more belief in God's Mercy and Compassion.

You will have a more active prefrontal cortex by keeping the mind active on positive affirmations.

The science behind affirmations in neurological terms is clearly an up-regulation. The prefrontal cortex ensures the hypothalamus produces more serotonin.

More Serotonin ensures a more active prefrontal cortex.

A positive fuelling for change allows you to see a clearer path towards that best version of you as one of God's own.

Affirmations are positive statements of intent a gateway to becoming kinder to yourself, especially to those who self-harm or are too hard on themselves.

Disciplining ourselves to think act and interact with the world around us more positively.

Choosing to start your day in a more positive frame of mind starting your day with a positive intention with God.

Affirmations promote the intention to change for the better in any area of your life, especially which may be in lack.

Affirmations can reinforce the belief that you can get past your current hardship and look forward to a brighter future god is with you always.

Affirmations replace outdated limited beliefs becoming progressively easier to create what you want in life.

Daily affirmations help you vibrate in alignment with abundance rather than lack.

Positive Affirmations reconnect you with feelings of Gratitude for all that God is doing for you in the present moment.

Affirmations are like exercises for our mind and outlook and improve our chances of success.

Affirmations can be used as a treatment and works well alongside other treatments thus complementing it.

It may take some time to notice any changes so patience will be required and persistence to reach the desired outcome.

Take back control of your thoughts and begin altering these thought patterns.

Altering these thought patterns produce a positive outlook and you become more focused on your creator.

You may want to use affirmations to control negative feelings.

Improve your productivity or keep your motivation.

You may want to use these affirmations for behaviour change and use these affirmations to assist you in that process.

Affirmations are a self-help tool for a successful Strategy.

Affirmations can help strengthen self-worth by boosting your positive opinion of yourself.

Use these affirmations for god focusing on these positive statements to promote self-confidence.

Affirmations generally work as a tool for shifting your mindset.

Affirmations help you to achieve your goals.

Affirmations encourage your brain to take these positive affirmations as fact with true belief.

Believing in your own ability with God's help and assistance reminds you that you are not alone.

There is indeed a higher source that we can use in a positive way to boost optimism and improve mood.

Allowing yourself to focus away from perceived failure and inadequacies directing your focus toward God's given Strengths to you.

Practising affirmations may help you feel more relaxed and help you get through stressful moments.

You may want to add these affirmations after prayer.

Affirmations then are serving as an additional resource.

Affirmations can be used to help you overcome self-doubt decrease stress and become more open to behaviour change and a positive outlook.

Affirmation may broaden your overall perception of what God thinks of you rather than what others think or say about you.

Affirmations can reduce the effects of negative emotions reducing reactivity and regulating emotions.

Self-affirmations work by priming the regions of the ventrolateral prefrontal cortex.

Affirmations are effective due to Neuroplasticity or the re-wiring of the brain.

Our brains are constantly re-wiring themselves and building new neural pathways.

Affirmations are one way to re-wire to think more positive.

Positive affirmations tell us that we are still doing well and that we should not give up hope.

Affirmations can give us build the momentum to not give up hope helping us build resilience and giving us an extra boost.

Affirmations can prevent us from ruminating over negative thoughts and situations.

Affirmations can encourage positive happy feelings thoughts and attitudes God intends us to be Joyful.

Affirmations challenge unhelpful thinking and are a helpful resource when you need support and reassurance from God this may reduce your sensitivity to threats.

Affirmations help build awareness support your well-being and encourage emotional stability.
Affirmations can inspire creativity and breakthrough limiting beliefs instilling hope for the future and encouraging a sense of calm helping you to be present with God at that moment.
Affirmations help you overcome inner barriers.

Affirmations create a positive perception of who you are and instil more belief in God's Mercy and Compassion.
You will have a more active prefrontal cortex by keeping the mind active on positive affirmations.
The science behind affirmations in neurological terms is clearly an up-regulation. The prefrontal cortex ensures the hypothalamus produces more serotonin.
More Serotonin ensures a more active prefrontal cortex.

A positive fuelling for change allows you to see a clearer path towards that best version of you as one of God's own.

Affirmations are positive statements of intent a gateway to becoming kinder to yourself, especially to those who self-harm or are too hard on themselves.

Disciplining ourselves to think act and interact with the world around us more positively.

Choosing to start your day in a more positive frame of mind starting your day with a positive intention with God.

Affirmations promote the intention to change for the better in any area of your life, especially which may be in lack.

Affirmations can reinforce the belief that you can get past your current hardship and look forward to a brighter future god is with you always.

Affirmations replace outdated limited beliefs becoming progressively easier to create what you want in life.

Daily affirmations help you vibrate in alignment with abundance rather than lack.

Positive Affirmations reconnect you with feelings of Gratitude for all that God is doing for you in the present moment.

Affirmations help you to enhance your perception of good things in life this can boost your happiness as well as raise your vibrational frequency.

Affirmations help you believe you are the kind of person that attracts good things that comes from God.

What you receive from God is not based on self-merit but purely because God Loves you.

These Affirmations can be said anywhere at any time at your own convenience.

It is recommended that you repeat an affirmation 1000 times a day or as much as you possibly can.

Alternatively, repeat an affirmation a day throughout the day and when as many times as possible.

This will boost your motivation and confidence strengthening your belief in the affirmations.

Take charge of your thoughts with intention of receiving the desired outcome you want. Practise consistently exercising persistence and patience as this process takes time.

Affirmations help you to enhance your perception of good things in life this can boost your happiness as well as raise your vibrational frequency.

Affirmations help you believe you are the kind of person that attracts good things that comes from God.

What you receive from God is not based on self-merit but purely because God Loves you.

These Affirmations can be said anywhere at any time at your own convenience.

It is recommended that you repeat an affirmation 1000 times a day or as much as you possibly can.

Alternatively, repeat an affirmation a day throughout the day and when as many times as possible.

This will boost your motivation and confidence strengthening your belief in the affirmations.

Take charge of your thoughts with intention of receiving the desired outcome you want. Practise consistently exercising persistence and patience as this process takes time.

Acknowledgement

Thank you to my Christian mother for the suggestion that I release my photographs of the landscape for the book
Thank you to interfaith charity for the multicultural events held locally

Thank you to jake for the technical support for book writing online
Thank you to John Academy for knowledge on personal development and for qualifying me

Why Repeat Affirmations

Here are a number of reasons for practising affirmations some of which are:

Believing that what you want is already on its way to you.
To be used as a convincing yourself tool.
Help you have a stronger force in your life.
You will gently return your focus and makes for more effective learning practising becoming more mindful and practising deliberately paying attention a way of improving your memory you are more likely to remember.
The more you start to believe the positive affirmation It can reinforce your value and self-worth.
Repeating with enthusiasm and love can help brighten your outlook on the world.
Easier to maintain a positive attitude.
Builds the affirmation into your subconscious.
To help maintain Focus.
Helps to absorb the affirmations.
Uplifts your mood.
Keeps you positive throughout the day.
More positive affirmations spoken each day the less room for negative thought.

Suggestions on how to apply Affirmations

1. Write out an affirmation several times in a notebook and carry it with you.

2. Repeat the affirmations as often as you can throughout the day.

3. Use positive affirmations while Meditating.

4. Write affirmations on a sticky note and place them around your house and or office as a reminder to say the affirmations.

5. Repeat affirmation as soon as you engage in a negative thought.

6. Take three deep breaths then say slowly and clearly say the affirmation and allow your body to relax.

7. Absorb the positive feeling of the affirmation.

8. Start your day with adding affirmations to your daily routine.

9. Pick one affirmation to repeat throughout the day.

10. Smile after saying positive affirmations as a smile helps the brain accept the affirmations without trying to challenge it so much.

11. set aside a time to dedicate to your affirmation.

12. Act as if the thing you are affirming is your reality —like you have already achieved whatever it is.

Words of Encouragement

Train your Subconscious mind away from limiting and often damaging beliefs and introduce more positive ones by repeating Affirmations.

Flooding the mind with positive thoughts and positive beliefs you
want particularly right before sleep and as soon as you wake up these are the times when your subconscious mind is most receptive.

I encourage you to use these Affirmations as a Personal intervention focusing on
empowering you to Godly change and have a positive way of life a lifestyle choice.
Repeating these affirmations has positive benefits and is a powerful tool for personal transformation using a consistent approach.

These affirmations are not of any religious denomination and are Godly universal you may have a basic belief that God exists or you may be open to believing.
I hope you enjoy the process of affirmation in this book and you feel loved comforted supported and nurtured.

God Bless!

Lets Start

God is giving me the

energy to carry out

my tasks

today

God is lifting

my self-esteem

to a higher plane

today

God's abundant

energy is

flowing through

me today

God is with me

so I am joyful

today

God is

my

higher source

God is motivating

me to do my

best today

God is

with me

I am happy

today

God has

my best interests

at

heart

God is

with me

I feel confident today

God is

helping me

become more
Compassionate

God loves me

unconditionally today

and every day

God's love dwells

within

me

everyday

God puts

me first

all the

time

God is motivating me

today so I feel motivated

Today I take my

problems to God

in prayer

With God

nothing

is

Impossible

Love in

my heart

comes

from

God

I dwell in

God's presence

all the

time

God keeps me

safe all

the

time

With God I

am Loveable kind

and

gentle

With God

I

*am capable
and productive*

*I can do all
things
through
God*

*I am a
child
of God
every
day*

*God is involved
in everything
I do*

I serve
God
by
serving others
I am
in
God's
hands
alone

*God has a great plan
for my
life*

*God teaches
me divine
words*

*God listens to
my prayers*

*God is on my
side all the time*

*God is in
control of my
life*

*God has found a
place in my heart
and mind*

*God has a special
place in my
heart and soul*

*I am grateful
to god daily*

God's love
for me
is eternal

*God has forgiven
me of all the wrong
I have done*

God gives me Hope

There is hope with God

*God is teaching me
all the time*

*I am learning
about God
everyday*

*God is watching
over me with
humbleness*

*God is my
powerful
source*

God loves the World

*God showers me
with blessings*

*God is in my life
each day I am grateful*

*There is no greater
love than
God's Love for me*

God is for me
not against me

*God created me
for a good
purpose*

*God has a good plan
for me a fulfilling
life with an abundance*

I believe God loves me

God is in control

*God is giving me the
energy to carry out
my tasks
today*

*God is lifting my
self-esteem
to a higher plane
today*

God's abundant energy
is flowing through
me today

*God is
with me
so I am joyful
today*

God is
my
higher source

*God is motivating
me to
do my
best today*

*God is
with me
I am
happy
today*

God has
my best interests
at
heart

*God is
with me
I feel confident
today*

*God is
helping me
become more
Compassionate*

*God loves me
unconditionally
today and every day*

*God's love dwells
within
me
everyday*

*God puts
me first
all the
time*

*God is motivating me
today so I feel motivated*

*Today I take my
problems to God
in prayer*

With God nothing is Impossible

*Love in
my heart
comes
from
God*

I dwell in
God's presence
all the
time

*God keeps me
safe all
the
time*

*With God I
am Loveable kind
and
gentle*

With God
I
am capable
and productive

*I can do all
things
through
God*

I am a
child
of God
every
day

*God is involved
in everything
I do*

I serve
God
by
serving others

*I am
in
God's
hands
alone*

*God has a great
plan
for my
life*

*God teaches
me divine
words*

God listens to
my prayers

God is on my
side all the time

*God is in
control of my
life*

*God has found
a place in my
heart and mind*

*God has a special
place in my heart
and soul*

I am grateful to god daily

*God's love
for me
is eternal*

*God has forgiven me of
all the wrong
I have done*

God gives me Hope

There is hope with God

*God is teaching
me all the time*

*I am learning
about God
everyday*

*God is watching
over me with
compassion*

*God is my
powerful
source always*

God loves all of me

*God showers me
with love*

*God is in my life
each day I am
loved*

*There is no greater
love than
God's Love for me
and those I know*

God is for me
not against me
God encourages me

*God created me
for a kind
purpose*

God has a good plan
for me for a
fulfilling life in truth

God loves me

*God is in control
of my life*